How to Get to Awesome

101 WAYS TO

FIND YOUR BEST SELF

Rhonda Sciortino

hatherleigh
Improve your life. Change your world.

Improve your life. Change your world.

Hatherleigh Press is committed to preserving and protecting the
natural resources of the earth. Environmentally responsible
and sustainable practices are embraced within the
company's mission statement.

Visit us at www.hatherleighpress.com and register online for free
offers, discounts, special events, and more.

How to Get to Awesome
Text copyright © 2016 Rhonda Sciortino

Library of Congress Cataloging-in-Publication Data is available upon
request.
ISBN: 978-1-57826-635-7

Interior and cover design by Cynthia Dunne

Printed in the United States
10 9 8 7 6 5 4 3 2 1

To Dominic and Luca,
the two most awesome people on Earth.

Contents

❋

Introduction: What is "Awesome"? • 1

Awesome people choose to be optimistic • 11

Awesome people are purposeful • 23

Awesome people are honest • 35

Awesome people are generous • 47

Awesome people are good leaders • 59

Awesome people value good relationships • 71

Awesome people are responsible • 83

Awesome people are good communicators • 95

Awesome people are resourceful • 107

Awesome people are effective • 119

Step #101 to Awesomeness • 131

Conclusion • 133

About the Author • 138

CHARACTERISTIC #1	Awesome people choose to be optimistic.
CHARACTERISTIC #2	Awesome people are purposeful.
CHARACTERISTIC #3	Awesome people are honest.
CHARACTERISTIC #4	Awesome people are generous.
CHARACTERISTIC #5	Awesome people are good leaders.
CHARACTERISTIC #6	Awesome people value good relationships.
CHARACTERISTIC #7	Awesome people are responsible.
CHARACTERISTIC #8	Awesome people are good communicators.
CHARACTERISTIC #9	Awesome people are resourceful.
CHARACTERISTIC #10	Awesome people are effective.

INTRODUCTION:
WHAT IS "AWESOME"?

AWESOMENESS IS NOT only a frame of mind; it is a way of being. It is an attitude. It is a journey that, along the way, becomes a lifestyle. Ultimately, awesomeness is a destination. Awesome people have, well, an awesomeness about them. The word "awesome" is an adjective, defined as "causing or inducing awe; inspiring an overwhelming feeling of reverence, admiration, or fear, as in "an awesome sight." More recently, the word "awesome," used as slang, has come to mean "very impressive" or "terrific," as in "a job well done." This book is designed to take "awesome" to a new level, by introducing you to "awesome" as a verb!

The great news is that every one of us can get to "awesome," because awesomeness is already in us. Every day can be awesome. That doesn't mean that we will always be happy, that we will never feel sad or that only good things will happen to us. It does mean that we can experience awesomeness every day of our lives, regardless of our circumstances. Unfortunately, so many of us have experienced bumps on the road of life that have disconnected us from the incomparable feeling of awesome. After so many difficulties, we can become so disconnected from awesomeness that we forget it even exists.

Sadly, some people have never even experienced the feeling of awesomeness. These people have gone through life feeling like the last kid that no one picked for sports teams in school. It feels awful to be the one unwanted by either team, especially while the awesome ones are wanted by both teams, and the exceptionally awesome "cool kids" are the natural selections as the "team captains". Some people feel like they're anything but awesome, and they've had experiences that back up that feeling. They feel like the kids who walked home alone after school while the awesome kids hung out with the "popular kids," or went to their music lessons, or to sports practices, or to some other awesome activity from which they've been excluded.

The "unawesome" people are those who feel like spectators in life, standing by and watching those who are awesome (and who know it) get all the good things in life. These are the people who seem to always get the best jobs, marry the right spouses, buy houses in the nicest neighborhoods, and who start the cycle all over again by having the perfect children, for whom everything is provided for. In other words, these are the ones who are born awesome…the ones who have it made.

What the "unawesome" people don't yet know is that

everyone has the potential and the capacity to become awesome. Although you may not feel it's possible now, you have within you your own unique brand of awesomeness and you can become a participant in life and not just a spectator!

Keep in mind that everyone has their problems—even the awesome people. Not one of those seemingly awesome people has it as perfectly as it may appear. Their families aren't perfect. They aren't immune to sickness. They aren't exempt from growing old. There isn't a force field around them that protects them from tragedy. But despite the fact that awesome people can experience the pain of divorce, death of a loved one, financial ruin, or any of the other things that can and do happen, the awesome people do seem to be able to make it through the inevitable challenges of life relatively unscathed, with their awesomeness intact.

The "unawesome" ones, who weren't born into awesomeness, can't quite put their finger on what it is that makes some people awesome (and what makes others not quite so). The differences between the cool and the uncool, the awesome and the unawesome, have been a mystery—that is, until now!

No longer will those who feel "unawesome" have to go through life with the vague sense that they are not quite good enough, or worse, that they're too broken to be repaired. The truth is there is awesomeness inside each of us! Those of us who don't feel awesome just aren't aware of our awesomeness—yet.

Most people don't know what, specifically, contributes to awesomeness, so they carry around aspects of awesomeness and aren't even aware of it. They don't act like the awesome people they truly are and the confident people they could be. Consequently, they miss out, and don't get as much out of life as they should.

Some people even go through life with a chip (or a cement block) on their shoulder, eaten up by feelings of envy toward others who seem to have gotten all the advantages. They feel like they were dealt a bad hand at the game of life; like they're owed restitution by someone, somehow, but they go through life never quite able to figure out how and where to collect.

Those poor souls with the chips on their shoulders wish they'd been born into a loving family, or that Dad hadn't left, or that Mom hadn't lost her job. They wish they'd lived in a home that they weren't ashamed of—a home where they could've had friends over. They wish they had gotten a better education. They wish they'd had it as good as those awesome kids. They wish… they wish… they wish…but none of those wishes will ever change their present reality. No one can go back in time and choose a different family through which to enter into life. No one can change where they grew up, what happened, or what they didn't get but should have.

The good news is that awesomeness is not a prize awarded at birth to only a select few, never to be attained by anyone else. Awesomeness is attainable by each of us. Every one of us can embark today on a journey toward our own awesome lifestyle. It's not difficult. But it is a commitment to a shift in attitude.

Each of us is able to tease out and identify those things that make us awesome. We can develop each characteristic of awesomeness by doing every step in this book until one day we realize that we've become who we want to be, and that we're living the life we want to live. Somewhere along our journey toward the destination of awesomeness, we can brush the chips off our shoulders, and see ourselves in a whole new light as the awesome people we are—the awesome people we were always meant to be!

When that happens, no longer are we the unawesome ones left unchosen for the team. No longer must we stand at the sidelines as spectators, watching others play the game of life. No longer must we sit at home while others advance to ever-greater degrees of awesome.

This book identifies the 10 key characteristics that make people awesome. As you read these characteristics and their descriptions, you'll see yourself. You'll see that you have had awesomeness inside of you all along, and you will likely see areas that you can work on to become even more awesome.

Along with each of the 10 characteristics of awesomeness, you will find practical guidance for developing those characteristics and for applying them in every area of your life. This advice is broken down into 10 steps that will help you develop, strengthen, and hone each characteristic. The great thing is that every step of the journey to awesome is an easy, free, and simple way that you can nurture the characteristics of awesomeness, and in so doing transform yourself and the quality of your life.

The 101st step to becoming your best self follows the last step of the 10th characteristic. This one last step will place you at the threshold of your ultimate destination of awesomeness!

Reading about each characteristic and taking each of the steps toward realization of the characteristics of awesomeness that are outlined in this book is the price of admittance to the destination of awesomeness. Is it work? Yes. Is it worth it? You better believe it! It's well worth the investment!

If you follow the steps of this journey from beginning to end, you will discover that you are truly awesome and, more importantly, you will know why you are so. You'll recognize and value the combination of characteristics that make you awesome, and you will be confident in your own awesomeness. No, you won't become arrogant. You will become comfortable in your own skin—content with yourself in a way you may have never been.

You have a very special package of skills, talents, abilities, and characteristics that is unique in all the world. You may or may not be built to be the team captain, but it is certain that you were built to be the most awesome YOU than has ever existed in the history of humanity. Once you know what makes you awesome and you arrive at your destination of awesomeness, you will be the one everyone wants on their team!

You'll get along with others better than you ever have before. Why? Because you'll be able to confidently communicate who you are, what you care about, and what makes you awesome. Your awesomeness will attract other awesome people like a magnet! No longer will you feel badly about what you don't do well because your focus will be on your awesomeness, not on any perceived weaknesses. No longer will you envy the awesomeness of others because you will know that each person's special package of unique awesomeness is theirs and theirs alone.

You will know that each one of us is truly in a category of our own, not better or worse than anyone else, but unique and valuable, each in our own awesome way. Importantly, you'll know that when awesome people join together, each person's unique package of awesomeness beautifully fills the weak places of the other, allowing the two to accomplish more than either could on his or her own!

Even better, because you'll be able to recognize and celebrate the awesome characteristics in others, you'll be helping everyone within your influence to embark on their own journey toward awesomeness as well. When you find and point out the awesomeness of others, you help bring out the very best in them. Awesome people, and those who want to be awesome, will be drawn to you, opportunities will present themselves to you, and you'll find yourself in the midst of an immeasurably awesome life!

When you are confident in your awesomeness, living your awesome lifestyle, you'll be more willing to step out to try new things, meet new people, and attempt things you may never have had the courage to try before. When you're living awesomely, you will really live, with a vibrancy that you have never experienced before.

You may want to consider journaling as you progress on your path to awesomeness. Note the awesome qualities you discover about yourself. Note the ways you can become even more awesome. Write down ideas that come to mind for things that you dare to see as possible for you. Consider creating an ongoing action list of people to call, letters to write, and ideas to share. As you progress on your journey, your notes will inspire you, your confidence will grow, and you just may find that ideas shared spark an exciting future that you never would have believed was possible.

So, get ready, suspend any doubt or skepticism, and let's embark on the journey to your destination of AWESOME!

Awesome people choose to be optimistic

AWESOME PEOPLE KNOW that they can choose to expect things to work out well or to go terribly wrong. This doesn't mean that optimistic people don't have problems, that they are naturally positive, or that they automatically see things through rose-colored glasses. Rather, they know that they are more likely to do what's necessary to cooperate and collaborate toward a good resolution (and to get others to do the same) if they approach the challenges of life with the expectation that everything will somehow, some way, work out.

Choose to look for the possibility for good in every challenge.

When you're looking for good, you are more likely to find it and you'll enjoy the journey of life more because your attitude will be more positive. Awesome people are happy! Of course, this doesn't mean that awesome people never feel sadness or that sad things don't happen to awesome people. Rather, when they *do* feel sadness, they go through it; they keep moving forward until they come out on the other side, choosing once again to be happy. They know that happiness is a choice—a matter of attitude. Their happiness does not disintegrate when they are cut off in traffic or overlooked for a promotion. Awesome people choose not to allow anyone or any circumstance to take away their happiness. They simply choose not to give anyone that much power over their lives.

When you feel unhappy, retrace your steps until you figure out what led to you feeling this way.

If you find that you are in a bad mood after eating or drinking something, eliminate or cut back on the offending substance (such as alcohol, sugar, gluten, etc.) in the future. If you were with someone who is negative, limit your time with that person in the future. If you feel unhappy because of circumstances that are outside of your control, remind yourself that the situation is only temporary. Keep moving forward through the difficulty with a smile on your face, and you will eventually come out on the other end to your choice of happiness again.

You cannot be optimistic and negative at the same time.

You can be one or the other, but not both. Being optimistic is a *choice*; it is not simply a personality characteristic that you either have or don't have. Optimism is nurtured and developed until eventually it comes naturally. To become and remain optimistic, stop saying anything that is critical or otherwise negative about people, places, or situations. When a negative thought comes into your mind, *stop*. Either rephrase the comment in a positive way (if possible), or don't say anything. This process lets you learn how to apply a filter to your thoughts. Awesome, optimistic people do not allow every thought that pops into their heads to fall out of their mouths.

It is inevitable that you'll face challenges in life.

Everyone does. Although those challenges can be painful and even life changing, keep in mind that you *always* have options. Awesome people know that although their lives can change dramatically because of things that are outside of their control, what *is* in their control is their response to the situation. They know that they have the ability to create a "new normal." They know that their lives may never be the same as they once were, but that they can move beyond the challenge and be okay. Awesome, optimistic people know that it is possible to grow because of the challenging times of their lives, and ultimately be better off than they were before the challenge.

Decide to celebrate life!

Awesome people smile, not only because they feel like it, but also because they deliberately *choose* to smile. When we smile, beneficial chemicals are released in our brains, which can actually help us feel better. The more we smile, the better we feel. Our intentional smiles remind us, and everyone around us, that we believe that there will be brighter days ahead, that the best is yet to happen, and that difficult times do not last forever unless we allow them to. So don't wait until you feel happy to smile. Go ahead and smile first—your feelings will eventually catch up!

When was the last time you were enthusiastic about something?

For many people, it's been too long. Find something that you can be optimistic, or maybe even passionate, about. Is it volunteering to help someone in need? Is it a hobby you haven't touched in years? Is it an activity you haven't had time for? Connect with your enthusiasm or passion, and optimism will come easier to you. The more you engage with the passion inside you, the more optimistic you will become.

Laugh!

Laughter is good medicine—literally. When we laugh, tense muscles relax, natural anti-depressants are released, and challenges are set aside—at least for the moment. Find comics, podcasts, or videos that make you laugh, and keep them handy. Don't passively wait for someone or something to make you laugh. Make a point of helping yourself to enjoy a good belly laugh at least once a day. Laughter is infectious. It brightens the room you're in and lightens the mood. So go ahead, take your medicine; it encourages others to take theirs!

Be on the lookout for good characteristics and achievements in others.

When you see a good behavior or attitude, comment on it. We will see more of the good we want in the world when we recognize and celebrate positive behaviors and attitudes. This is especially true with children. They will often rise to our expectations (or sadly, they will lower themselves to negative expectations), so raise the bar for the young people within your influence by telling them specifically how and why you think they're awesome. The world around them (including other kids, movies, TV, and music) gives them messages about who they are, and those messages are not always positive. Make it your job to be the one who tells them about the awesome people they truly are before they start believing negative messages.

STEP 9

Be genuine and sincere.

Awesome people know that there is no room for deceit in authentic optimism. People sometimes use "little white lies" to save the feelings of others, to avoid conflict, or to save time. The reality is that being disingenuous or insincere doesn't help anyone. For example, telling someone that they look fine when they have spinach covering their two front teeth doesn't do them any favors. It may save them from momentary embarrassment, but it can lead to exponentially larger humiliation. Even when you have to deliver difficult information, learn to do it with good-natured optimism and gentleness. When you do that, you earn the trust of others, and you are better able to maintain your sense of hope for a good future while helping others gain and maintain theirs.

Most of the worries that chip away at our sense of optimism never actually occur.

Rather than worry about things that aren't likely to happen anyway, envision a back-up scenario in case your concern actually does happen. Then choose to believe that no matter what happens, you'll still be awesome, and your awesomeness and optimism will attract other good things to come your way.

Awesome people are purposeful

AWESOME PEOPLE WANT to feel the fulfillment and contentment that comes from a life well lived. Awesome people are deliberate about the choices they make, and are careful not to do anything that would distract them from fulfilling their purpose. They are content with their strengths; they are humble and authentic, acknowledging their weaknesses. They don't waste time trying to be good at everything. Rather, they focus on making their good qualities great. They surround themselves with other awesome people who are strong where they are weak. By doing that, they draw the greatness out of others, and help them to become the best they can be. Awesome people know that they were perfectly matched to the purpose of their lives, and have—or have access to—all they need to fulfill it.

**Consider what you would like to do
if you knew you only had
six months left to live.**

The answer to this question likely has something to do with your passion and purpose. If you know your purpose, are you actively working towards it? Or does life always get in the way? If you don't know your purpose, ask yourself what you feel strongly about. Ask what you're passionate about, and explore the dream in your heart. Once you know what you would focus on in your last days, you'll have more clarity about what you want to do purposely with every day between now and then.

Make a list of your strengths, natural talents, learned skills, and the personality characteristics that make you who you are.

If you're not sure about your strengths, consider taking an online assessment or asking yourself questions like, "Am I patient, kind, strong?" "Am I a good listener?" "Am I problem solver?" "Am I good at fixing things?" Most people who are naturally good at something tend to assume that everyone is good at it. After all, it comes so easily to them. Nevertheless, the truth is that your particular talent or the way you see and interpret things may be a gift that others don't have. Believe that whatever combination of assets you possess is specifically what you need to fulfill the good plan for your life. When you recognize the unique package of assets that make you awesome, you are better able to use and even leverage those assets to purposefully create the awesome life you want to live!

STEP 13

Knowing what you're good at and what you're not so good at accomplishes two things.

First, it helps you to better communicate your strengths to employers, colleagues, and to those closest to you so that you are better understood, and so that others can manage their expectations of you. Secondly, it also helps you to gain confidence while remaining humble and authentic. When we know what we're good at, we don't have to be jealous of the abilities of others. We are confident in our own abilities. We can recognize and celebrate the skills of others because we know that although they are genius in their own unique way, there are areas in which they privately struggle. No one is good at everything. Awesome people don't have to try to pretend that they're something they're not because they know that everyone has skills in the areas in which they shine. As you learn to communicate those qualities that make you awesome, you'll become more comfortable with being your authentic self.

Value the strengths of others by looking for them, pointing them out, and rewarding them with a compliment.

When you do that, you will get more of the behavior you recognize and celebrate. Family members, co-workers, and everyone else in your life will begin to try to live up to your compliments. Valuing others affirms them and helps to build their self-esteem. They will appreciate you for seeing the good in them, and they'll be far more likely to take advice from you because they will know that you value them.

Once you know what you're good at and you have a sense of your unique purpose, focus on doing it!

Refuse to be distracted by every new activity and opportunity that presents itself. Not every good opportunity is necessarily a good option for you. When an opportunity presents itself, ask yourself if the new opportunity fits with your purpose. If not, don't do it. If it does, do it with reckless abandon. Create a strategy for doing something every day that moves you closer to the fulfillment of your purpose.

**STEP
16**

Believe in your purpose and in your ability to fulfill it.

Refuse to give up on fulfilling your purpose just because something doesn't turn out the way you thought it would, or within the timeframe you had hoped for. Awesome people are persistent. They understand that the game of life is a game of endurance. It's a marathon, not a sprint. So, rather than set their purpose aside when it becomes difficult, they refuse to take the easy route of slipping back into mediocrity. Even if they take three steps forward and two steps back, they continue taking those steps, one by one. Awesome, purposeful people know that with every attempt to move forward, they move closer to living their ideal awesome life.

In order to live a life of continuous progression toward the fulfillment of your purpose, you must develop the ability to persuade others of the things you believe in.

Of course, not everyone will go along with you, and in those cases, it's wise to agree to disagree rather than lose your peace by attempting to force the other person to see things your way. Purposeful people know that persuasion never involves force. Awesome, purposeful people attempt to persuade others to cooperate and collaborate with them by helping them understand that what they are suggesting is in the best interests of everyone involved. Importantly, awesome people know that if a situation isn't good for everyone, it isn't good for anyone.

**Avoid impulsive decisions
and behaviors.**

For example, if you've decided to spend your Saturday reading up on a subject that will help you prepare for an important meeting the following week, but a friend calls and invites you to go to the movies, the purposeful response is to explain to your friend that you'd love to go a different day, but cannot do it today. An impulsive person would kick their plans to the curb in favor of the movies without giving their important meeting another thought. The purposeful person stands firm on the decision to do the reading necessary to advance their career. Impulsive people are easily distracted from their purpose, and thus live their whole lives never having fulfilled their purpose or enjoying the sense of satisfaction that comes with it.

Purposeful people, by definition, are determined to accomplish the goal they set for themselves.

They have a dogged determination to make it no matter what challenges or setbacks they encounter. Regardless of where you're from, what you've been through, or what you're going through now, decide right now that you absolutely refuse to be deterred or distracted from finding and fulfilling your purpose, the purpose for which you were born. Awesome, purposeful people determine to live their uniquely awesome life. Do that, and before you know it you'll be living the life you were born to enjoy!

In following all these steps toward living an awesome, purposeful life, you will develop an indomitable spirit.

The indomitable spirit rolls all these traits into one characteristic. Challenges will arise, but if you continue following these steps, you will build up within you a determined, persistent, persuasive, strategic, confident, indomitable spirit. So think of the challenges you face on your journey toward awesome as sandpaper that rubs the rough edges off you, and polishes you to a shine that can never be dulled. And if you fail at a specific endeavor, think of it as falling off a bicycle. You didn't put the bike in the trash heap and never rode again. You got up, brushed yourself off, and got back on the bike. Don't be afraid to fail. Failure provides invaluable insight on what does not work. When you fail at something, do what awesome people do: ignore the scoffers, mine the lessons out of it, come up with a different approach, and try again.

Awesome people are honest

AWESOME PEOPLE KNOW that dishonesty does not serve them. Some lies are designed to make us look better, like, "I'm sorry I am late—there was a lot of traffic," when the real reason for the tardiness is you woke up late. Some lies are told to avoid hurting someone's feelings. For example, someone asks if you like her new outfit, and you think it's unflattering, but say, "You look terrific." Awesome people know that there is no substitute for honesty. They have learned how to apologize for tardiness without providing personal information, and how to find something good to say without lying or hurting the feelings of others. Awesome people earn a reputation for being truthful and trustworthy, characteristics that are highly valued.

Henry Ford, founder of the Ford Motor Company, is credited with saying, "Never complain, never explain."

When you are late to work or to a social engagement, acknowledge the fact with an apology, but unless specifically asked, don't offer a lengthy explanation. If everything is already behind schedule, taking the time to offer an unsolicited, detailed explanation will only make matters worse. If you know in advance that you're going to be late, call ahead with an apology offering something like, "Something has come up, so I'll be late, but I will be there." If pressed for an explanation, give a truthful answer in as succinct a way as possible. Everyone has experienced some kind of problem getting out of the house in the morning. Awesome people are confident enough in themselves to be truthful, to offer to make it up to the person, and then to skillfully and gracefully redirect the conversation back to the matters at hand.

STEP 22

Avoid the "little white lie" myth.

Many people assume that it's acceptable to lie about things that (seemingly) have no consequence—like telling someone you like their outfit when you think it's hideous. Learn to speak with gentle honesty like, "My favorite is that blue outfit you wore last week. It looks amazing on you." When asked about someone's hairstyle, you could say something like, "I think you look terrific when your hair frames your face." Rather than saying that they look terrible, learn to compliment the person on something else entirely. If the person persists in asking for a direct answer to their question, give a facial expression that would suggest what you are trying not to say. Sometimes an expression is worth a thousand words. If you are pressed into a direct statement, state your opinion as kindly as possible along with a positive reference. For example, "To be totally candid, this hairstyle isn't my favorite. I liked it the way you used to wear it."

Some people lie to promote themselves.

These are the exaggerations that many people use to make themselves look better. It's called "Reputation Management." A colorful exaggeration when telling a story can be okay, as long as you say something like, "Of course, I'm exaggerating to make a point." However, exaggerations on a resume are never acceptable. Awesome people resist the temptation to make themselves look better by instead learning how best to emphasize their unique combination of strengths, talents, and abilities. When you know what makes you awesome, you have no need for the lies that attempt to elevate you. In truth, all these lies do is lower you in the eyes of others when the exaggeration is uncovered—and it will always eventually be uncovered.

Some people lie because they're ashamed of the truth.

They may have been victims of a personal violation, like a violent crime, or they're ashamed of an addiction or of bad choices they've made in the past. Awesome people know that there is no shame in being victimized by someone who violated them. They know that even their own past choices don't have to define them *unless they allow it.* The key to dealing with lies stemming from shame is to get the help you need to deal with it and then to move beyond it. Many people have been victimized. Many people have made bad choices in their past. Awesome people don't allow the events of the past to determine their future. They learn to tell the part of the truth they are comfortable sharing, explain that they're working on it, and then change the subject. No one is perfect. Everyone could use improvement. Awesome people are on a life-long journey towards ever-increasing awesomeness!

**Don't make the mistake of lying
to avoid the consequences of something.**

Kids lie about having broken a rule to avoid punishment. Some people lie to the police officer who pulled them over about how fast they were going in the hopes that they won't get a citation for speeding. Own your choices. Awesome people make choices knowing what the positive rewards or negative consequences may be. Awesome people own their choices and are prepared to enjoy whatever reward or accept whatever consequence may result. When you are truthful about your choices, and are clear about the possible consequences, you'll have no need to lie.

STEP 26

Some people are dishonest about things in an attempt to persuade someone else to act.

Sales people who exaggerate the benefits of a product or service do so to manipulate others into purchasing what they're trying to sell. Someone trying to persuade a friend to go along with something may say, "Of course we'll be home by 10," knowing in all honesty that they won't be home until after midnight. When you use deception to persuade others, you quickly destroy the good reputation you were working to build. One lie can result in others mistrusting everything you say or do. Think of it this way: injecting even one small lie into a relationship is like putting one tablespoon of poison in your iced tea. Yes, it's just a little. Nevertheless, the damage it can do can be catastrophic.

Some people engage in the lie of omission, which is telling a partial truth while failing to tell the whole truth.

In the case of someone who is asking for details just to be nosey, you have no obligation to give details that are personal, and that you do not wish to share. However, when you omit details of something that could be relevant in some way to the other person, you will earn the reputation for being less than truthful, even untrustworthy. Develop a habit of telling the truth, the whole truth, and nothing but the truth.

Some people speak of what they want to have happen in their lives as though it already happened.

Some people consider this a lie, and if the hoped-for thing never comes to fruition, then it is nothing more than deceit. However, if you accompany spoken goals with hard work and faith, you may just see these things become self-fulfilling prophecies in your life. For example, imagine the teenager who says, "Even though no one in my family has ever gone to college, I'm going to go until I get my doctorate. In fact, you can just start calling me 'Doctor' now!" If the teenager begins calling himself "Doctor" and encourages friends and family to do the same, he is far more likely to eventually achieve his goal. When you set goals for yourself, let people know that you are speaking of the things you want in your life in order to motivate yourself so that they don't dismiss your aspirational declarations as lying!

If you're going to make it a habit to speak the truth, you will also want to be able to hear the truth.

Ask for truthful feedback from others, and make it easy for them to give it to you. In other words, don't argue or become irritable when you hear something that suggests that you have done something wrong or that you need to improve. There's nothing wrong with setting the record straight in a calm manner, but don't make the mistake of doing so in an angry manner. Listening carefully to feedback from others, asking clarifying questions, and asking for and listening carefully to advice on how you can do better are signs of being teachable. Being offended or angry when someone offers criticism only reinforces the fact that you aren't yet able to handle the truth, and results in the unwillingness of people to tell you the truth in the future. Awesome people are on a lifelong journey of continuous learning and improvement. Make an effort to learn from everyone you meet—even if it's what *not* to do or how *not* to act.

Determine to be ethical and moral in everything you do.

Even if something is legal, it doesn't mean it's moral or ethical. Throughout history, there have been immoral laws. Don't assume that because something is legal, it's the right choice. If you make it a point to live in an honest, ethical, and moral way, you will develop a reputation for integrity that will attract good relationships and opportunities that you otherwise wouldn't have had. Avoid wrongdoing and the appearance of wrongdoing, even when you think no one is watching—and in these days of advanced technologies all around us, someone is always watching.

Awesome people are generous

AWESOME PEOPLE ARE more like flowing rivers than reservoirs. Most people think of generosity as having to do with money, and while that is one aspect of it, true generosity is so much more. Awesome people are generous with words of encouragement, praise, and gratitude. They are generous with their time—willing to help others in ways that use their unique strengths and skill sets. They are generous with their resources, especially with one of the most important of resources—wisdom. They give advice when solicited, and celebrate in the awesomeness developed in others. The great thing about generosity is that when you give to others, your goodness always eventually comes back to you.

Choose to believe that what you give comes back to you.

This is true for kindness, hope, wisdom, and every other good thing. It may not come back to you from the person you gave it to, but that doesn't matter. Your generosity *will* come back to you, sometimes from where you least expect it. Be generous, and see what happens.

STEP 32

Be generous with kindness.

It takes no extra time and costs nothing to give others a smile. Awesome people are not so inwardly focused that they fail to make eye contact with the people who cross their paths—especially those who can do nothing for them and nothing to them. For example, smile at the clerk behind the counter, say hello to the receptionist, acknowledge the stranger who holds the door open for you, and make eye contact and say "thank you" to the people you interact with throughout your daily life. In addition to enriching the lives of everyone within your influence, your life will be richer and more rewarding because of your generosity of kindness.

It is difficult to be generous with people who are grouchy, irritable, or just plain hard to get along with.

To better deal with difficult people, get up a few minutes earlier than usual. Use those minutes to close your eyes, get quiet, breathe deeply, and concentrate on peace. Ask peace to come into your life, and then go about your day. Those few minutes can set the tone for your entire day. If you feel yourself losing your peace, take a deep breath, hold it, exhale, and remind yourself to refuse to let anything steal, or interfere with, your peace. You can do the same thing with joy. This will allow you to be generous with your patience towards people who would otherwise ride on your last nerve! In the end, the ultimate benefit is yours because you'll be more focused on what everyone needs more of—peace and joy.

Be generous with your time.

When you sense that others are going through a tough time, be willing to listen if they want to talk or just spend time with them if they need some company. You don't have to fix the problem—it's probably out of anyone's control, anyway. Your time and genuine concern demonstrate compassion, which may just be the first step to awesome for the person who needs to be shown the way.

**Be generous with compassion
and empathy.**

Very often, the people we interact with throughout the day are fighting a battle that we're unaware of. You may not know that their spouse just left, that their teen is on drugs, or that they've just received a serious medical diagnosis. There are clues to the struggles of life. Some of the biggest clues to suffering are the very things that lead us to become angry, offended, or dismissive of others. For example, clues to private suffering often present themselves as mistakes, sadness, poor attitude, or a quietness that can be misinterpreted as being a snub or a slight. When someone acts in a way that you think is inappropriate, show compassion and empathy through a smile and a kind word.

**Generous people are poised
and gracious.**

They treat everyone with respect regardless of how others treat them. They are generous with care and concern for others. To be more poised, gracious, and caring of others, focus on others more than you do on yourself and your own needs. Oftentimes, considering the needs of others rather than focusing on our own problems can make us feel better.

Generous people are loyal.

In other words, they don't withdraw their generosity of kindness, time, or resources over a disagreement without first trying to work it out. They are faithful friends, ready to defend those who they perceive to be mistreated. They are especially protective of those who are most vulnerable. Be the awesome person who defends others and stands by them through thick and thin.

Awesome people are generous with their knowledge.

They are willing to teach others how to do something they've mastered. Be willing to take the time and expend the energy to teach someone how to do something that you know how to do. It will enrich the life of the other person, leaving an indelible imprint because of your generosity. This will often enrich the life of the awesome person as well, because awesomeness is like love—when you give it away, you get more in return. When you share your knowledge, don't be surprised if you learn something too.

**The next time you encounter a situation
in which you are tempted to handle
it forcefully, temper your approach
with gentleness, especially if there are
vulnerable people involved.**

Take a deep breath, and take a moment to consider who
is involved and where that person is emotionally. Begin
where he or she is, use a generous dose of gentleness,
and you'll have a much better resolution to the problem
at hand.

STEP 40

Be generous with your money.

A good financial rule to live by is to save some, spend some, and give some. Many people "give some" by giving to their church or charity of choice. They "spend some" by paying their bills. They "save some" by setting money aside for a rainy day or by investing in something they hope will reap financial rewards in the future. You may not always have money to give; when that is the case, look through your closet or garage for something else you can give. Perhaps there are people at the homeless shelter who desperately need those shoes you haven't worn in a year. There might be a young man in the community who is trying to start a gardening service who would make good use of that weed eater you used once. Awesome people enrich their lives and the lives of others by being givers.

Awesome people are good leaders

AWESOME PEOPLE TAKE the initiative to do what needs to be done. They understand that they are leaders to everyone within their influence, whether or not they are in traditional leadership positions at work or in the community. Awesome people know that everything they say and do is seen by others, and is an implied endorsement of that type of speech, behavior, and appearance. Therefore, awesome people carefully choose their words, behaviors, and appearance, as though everyone can see and hear what they're doing. This doesn't mean that they never misspeak or make a mistake, but it does mean that they take the mantle of leadership and their sphere of influence seriously, and that they intentionally act like the awesome people they aspire to be.

Awesome people know that they are being watched.

The things they say, their facial expressions, and their body language all tell a story. The pictures and comments they post on social media give further insight into their lives and their character. They are careful to dress, behave, and speak in a way that reflects the awesome, classy person they want to be known as. Awesome people only say and do things that reflect who they truly are. This doesn't mean that they don't occasionally say or do something they regret, but it means that when they do, they are quick to clear it up and eager to do better in the future.

Awesome people are aware that others are always paying attention to their words, attitudes, and behaviors, and that therefore they are always influencing the people around them—for good or for bad.

To be a positive influence (and to be a good leader), awesome people are careful to control their behaviors. They are careful to remain congruent and integrated. In other words, they are not one person on Saturday night and a completely different person on Sunday morning. They don't do or say things that they wouldn't want others to see. They have no need to try to be someone they're not because they know that their authentic self is awesome—not perfect, but uniquely awesome. Make sure that your words, attitudes, and actions reflect the person you want to be. Take off your mask and be the awesome person you really are. Those watching you will be influenced by your leadership and will follow in your footsteps toward awesomeness!

STEP 43

Leaders are resilient.

They're not afraid to take calculated risks because they know that failure at some attempted activity or venture doesn't make *them* a failure. It only means that the particular approach to the specific thing they tried didn't work. After a failed attempt, they step back, gather the facts, assess the data, and strategize for implementation of a different approach. You develop resilience by failing without allowing the failed attempt to damage you. Go ahead, try it—and keep on trying until you crack the code on your awesome ideas.

Awesome leaders are emotionally strong.

Despite the inevitable challenges of life, they continue to do what has to be done to take care of their responsibilities. When you face adversity, take a deep breath and calm your mind. Rather than facing a mountain of challenges all at once, list everything that has to be done. After you've made your list, prioritize each item in order of importance, and then tackle one thing at a time. This will help you maintain your strength during tough times.

Leaders are bold.

This doesn't mean they are obnoxious, but they are bold enough to ask directly for what they want. Leaders are especially bold when they're standing up for others—particularly for those who find it difficult to stand up for themselves. Everyone can learn to be bold and direct. The key is knowing the result you want, and then clearly communicating it.

Leaders are self-reliant.

They don't sit around waiting for others to take care of their needs. They don't rely on luck or good fortune. They take the initiative and do what they can to meet their own needs. Rather than asking others to do things that need to be done, do what you can to take care of your needs without harboring ill will towards the people who have fallen short of your expectations.

Leaders are independent.

This doesn't mean that they won't accept help when it's offered, or that they aren't cooperative and collaborative, or that they don't enjoy companionship. What it does mean is that they are capable of doing what they need to do, and of being content on their own. The more independent you are, the less dependent you'll be on others to meet your needs or to make you happy. This takes the pressure off others and puts the responsibility for ourselves squarely on our shoulders, where it belongs. The irony is that when we are independent, we attract other independent people into our lives who are often eager to help us reach our goals.

STEP 48

Leaders are courageous.

They have the courage to make a decision when others are paralyzed by fear or indecision. Leaders take calculated risks, and have the faith to try what they haven't tried before, accomplishing what has never been accomplished before. Awesome leaders are confident enough in themselves to attempt ventures that may reap huge rewards. Believe in yourself and in your purpose, and summon the courage inside you to step out in faith to achieve your goals.

Awesome leaders are creative.

They are willing to come up with ideas for possible solutions to challenges. They see difficulties as challenges and opportunities for positive resolution and growth rather than as potentially tragic problems. It requires confidence to let your creativity flow, to put forth ideas that come to mind to resolve difficulties. Every idea you have will not always make sense, and some may be downright absurd. Awesome people take the lead in putting out wild ideas to pave the way for others to have the freedom to share their ideas. You never know which idea will be a perfect solution or which idea will spark a thought in someone else's mind that leads to the ideal resolution or an amazing breakthrough.

Awesome leaders are aware of current events—in the world, in their community, in their family, and in their work.

They are typically voracious readers and/or learners. They often read or listen to subjects that are not directly related to them or to what they do. In this way, they broaden their perspective. They hear about how others solved problems in different families, cultures, and industries. They are then often able to extrapolate ideas and solutions for their issues from the totally unrelated problem solving of others. To be an awesome leader, read, listen, and pay attention to what's going on around you. People who make themselves knowledgeable and who build a broad perspective for themselves are the most highly valued people.

Awesome people value
good relationships

AWESOME PEOPLE ARE deliberate about surrounding themselves with others who encourage, inspire, and challenge them to rise higher. They limit their exposure to negative people, avoiding as much as possible those who are angry, bitter, resentful, or otherwise toxic. Awesome people invest the time and energy that's necessary to nurture good relationships.

Notice how you feel after spending time with some of the people in your life.

If you feel sad, angry, frustrated, or hurt after having been with someone, chances are their own issues have rubbed off on you. Try limiting your time with these people and you may find yourself better able to keep traveling toward awesome. If you cannot limit your time with them, develop selective hearing so that their negativity doesn't get in your head and heart. Either way, decide today that you refuse to take offense from anyone. Notice I said "*take* offense." Offensive comments can be hurled toward you, but you don't have to catch them. You can allow them to sail right past you. Offensive remarks reflect on the person who made them, not you. Don't let anyone bruise your awesomeness by catching and holding the offense they've lobbed at you. To do so only gives the offender a victory.

When you hear something negative about someone, don't automatically assume that it's true.

Rather, assume that it's not true until you know personally whether the ugly allegation is factual. Until you know with certainty about something, what you've heard is nothing more than gossip to be ignored. If you hear gossip or ugly comments about someone who isn't present, consider your options. First, you can ask the person who made the remark what evidence he or she has that their remark is factual. Second, you can make a declarative statement that you are unaware of anything having to do with the remark, and therefore have no opinion one way or the other. Then, change the subject. Third, you can refuse to listen to gossip by simply removing yourself from the conversation.

Act as though you love life and as though you have everything going for you.

Even if these things aren't yet true, act that way, and eventually they will become true for you. People who enjoy life attract others who want to enjoy their lives. Healthy relationships with positive people can develop from shared interests in good things and enjoyable activities. The more you act like you love your life, the sooner you actually will!

**STEP
54**

Think of patience as a verb.

Patience is something you must actively work towards—not just a trait you may or may not have. Patience is in all of us and can be developed in much the same way as a muscle is developed—through exercise. Intentionally invoke patience the next time you are tempted to become frustrated with someone. Refuse to say in anger or frustration the hurtful words that come to mind. We especially need to do this when we least feel like it. Awesome people know that they will accomplish much more if they wait to address the subject of their anger or frustration when everyone involved is calm and less agitated. With practice, having patience with people comes easier. The more patient we are, the more we show that we respect and value the person with whom we're being patient and that we place a high value on our own peace.

Awesome people deliberately look for reasons to compliment others.

They find the good and praise others for it. They're quick to compliment others, and with every compliment, they build on the relationship. They know that people will typically try to live up to the expectations of those who they believe genuinely like them. This practice of complimenting people isn't disingenuous, but is rather a sincere way of bringing out the best in others.

People draw closer to those who understand them.

So listen, *really* listen, to what others have to say. And while you're listening, watch. Watch for facial expressions, body language, and demeanor that may be clues to important things left unsaid. Many people feel that they can quickly summarize the problems after only a cursory listen to others. They jump in with advice, sometimes before even hearing what the person has to say. Often, people just need someone to talk to rather than someone to fix their problems. Awesome people actively listen, ask for clarification or anything that is unclear to them, and then say something like, "How do you think I may be of help?" This is not to suggest that awesome people don't give advice or offer helpful involvement. But it does mean that before offering advice, they ask, "May I offer some thoughts?" If you sense that they aren't receptive, don't take it personally. The comfort of the friendship and a willingness to listen may be all they need. So listen and try to understand their perspective.

STEP
57

Awesome people are slow to criticize others.

If they sense that someone is moving too fast down the wrong road toward inevitable danger, they'll intervene. But before assuming that they have all the facts and all the right answers, they'll ask questions, listen thoughtfully, gather information, and then draw conclusions before interjecting themselves. Awesome people would never criticize someone without having all the information and without having earned the right to give advice. Earn the right to give advice or bring correction through building good, healthy relationships.

**Awesome people are friendly
and sociable.**

Although they may withdraw for a time to deal with
challenges, trauma, or grief, they are willing to make
new friends and are consistent about maintaining good
relationships. Make time to get together with the people
you care about as well as with the people you'd like to
know better. When you are facing a challenging time, be
open to receiving comfort or help from others.

Awesome people are usually the first to ask forgiveness after a fight.

They are also quick to forgive others. They value other people and good relationships too much to allow disagreements or misunderstandings to create a divide between them. Awesome people will make their best case for their opinion and will listen carefully to the opinions of others. They can be very persuasive, but if after hearing each other out there is still disagreement, awesome people simply agree to disagree. They find areas on which they *do* agree, and focus more on what they have in common than on their differences. They refuse to allow differences of opinion to diminish their good relationships. Be quick to forgive and to accept the apologies of others.

Good relationships are those in which both people show their love.

Be aware that love may be shown in different ways. One person might verbally express their feelings while another might show it with physical touch like a hug or a hand on your shoulder. Others show love by gestures of kindness, such as sending a card or doing a special favor and still others show love by giving gifts. Don't expect others to show love the same way you do. For example, if you verbally tell loved ones how much you care about them, but they never say those things in return, don't assume they don't feel the same way. The other person may express love by some act of service like changing the oil in your car for you or fixing something around the house. Awesome people who value relationships give love freely and receive love in whatever way others are most comfortable in giving it.

Awesome people are responsible

AWESOME PEOPLE DO what they say they're going to do, when they say they're going to do it, or nearly die trying. They do what needs to be done without having to be told. When they make a mistake, they take responsibility and are willing to do whatever they can to make up for it. This highly developed sense of responsibility translates into every area of their lives—including relationships, work, health, and finances.

**STEP
61**

**Awesome people earn the reputation
of being reliable by doing what they
say they're going to do.**

Begin today to earn the reputation of being reliable by meaning what you say, and saying what you mean. For example, if you say you'll be there at 8 A.M., don't arrive at 8:15. If you're not sure if you can make it, say you're not sure. *Never* say that you'll do something and then change your mind later, or fail to show up because you no longer feel like doing what you committed to do. Don't make promises unless you're confident that you can keep them. A big part of building the reputation for being reliable is to learn to say "no" and stick to it. Don't say no only to be talked into it later. Don't agree to everything in an effort to keep people happy, which will only leave you feeling overcommitted, exhausted, and possibly even resentful. Saying yes to everything isn't what reliability is all about. If awesomely responsible people can't do something, they say clearly, "Thank you for the offer, but I am sorry to say that I can't."

STEP 62

Awesome people are stable, not flighty or flaky.

In other words, they're not friendly to everyone in the morning, and then rude or obnoxious in the afternoon. People like that are very difficult to be in a relationship with or to work with. You never know who they're going to be. People who are stable and consistent tend to maintain better relationships and longer-lasting employment. Awesome people decide to be stable by deliberately acting the same way toward others regardless of what they may be going through. Refuse to excuse your mistreatment of others. Determine to treat people courteously regardless of how you feel or what challenges you're facing.

STEP 63

Awesome people are temperate.

They never overindulge in food, wine, spending, or any of the other things that some people tend to overdo. Awesome people know that they will get more out of life if they enjoy their favorite things and experiences in moderation. They understand that if Christmas came around every month, it wouldn't be as special a celebration. Awesome people don't see being temperate as denying themselves. Rather, they see it as a way of keeping those things they enjoy as special—even precious—things. So the next time you're tempted to take a second helping, *stop*. Remind yourself that you are not denying yourself permanently—you can have more next time. Enjoy the anticipation of the thing you desire. After you've waited an appropriate length of time and you indulge in the thing you've looked forward to, you'll enjoy it that much more!

STEP 64

Awesome people are good at managing their money.

That doesn't always mean they have a lot of it, but it means that they know what they have, where it is, where it has to go and when, what they need to save, and what they have to spend. They know that if they go over their budget, they will have consequences in another area—the area for which that money was reserved. Before they make a purchase, they weigh out the advantages and disadvantages. They use common sense about purchases. If an item is going to be an expenditure with no chance of return on investment, they'll decline to make that purchase. On the other hand, if the item will help them earn more money, such as a vehicle that they'll use in business,, they'll make that investment. Awesome money managers do not make impulsive or emotional purchases. They always walk away, consider other options, do their research to make sure the purchase is a good one, and then negotiate their best deal. Manage your money or money will manage you.

STEP 65

Awesome people are intuitive at sensing needs.

They pay attention to the people around them. They know the typical behaviors of those they spend the most time with, so they can intuitively sense when something is wrong. This intuition comes naturally to some, but intuition is available to anyone who is willing to invest the time to develop the skills necessary to become intuitive about the thoughts and feelings of others. Being intuitive is a subtle characteristic of highly responsible people because it clues them in on what they can do to help a friend who is going through a rough time or to pick up the workload for someone who isn't feeling well. Intuitive, responsible people use their ever-developing intuition abilities, and then they offer relevant assistance, and in so doing they further build on their reputation for being responsible and reliable.

STEP 66

Responsible people are wise.

It's doesn't mean that they rank higher on the IQ scale than others, but it does mean that when they are in doubt about what needs to be done, they gather all available information, and then they use wisdom and common sense to make the best possible decisions. They use wisdom to choose which battles they'll fight, and which battles aren't worth fighting. They also use wisdom in choosing the right timing to act. Timing is an important part of serious discussions, big decisions, and implementation of strategic plans. Wise people know that it's never a good idea to have a serious conversation with someone who is distracted, working under a deadline, or not feeling well. You can best use wisdom and common sense when you're calm, cool, and collected. So do as the awesome responsible people do: keep your calm, gather all the data available to you, choose your battles, pick your timing, and achieve awesome results.

A big part of being responsible is being cautious—taking a proactive approach toward avoiding the bad things that <u>can</u> be avoided and lessening the impact of those bad things that cannot be avoided entirely.

Awesome people are careful to avoid preventable and foreseeable mistakes. They live by the old adage, "Measure twice and cut once." They know that people who act in haste, without gathering and assessing all the information, often make bad decisions. For example, they check the safety ratings before choosing a vehicle to purchase. They check the tire tread, fluid levels, and windshield wiper blades before taking a road trip. They check for traffic before choosing which route to take. They check online reviews before choosing a restaurant, dentist, or hairdresser. Awesome people know that they can avoid a lot of time consuming, costly, or even irreparable, consequences by doing their responsibly cautious due diligence ahead of time.

Responsible people are self-disciplined.

They don't have to be told what to do and how to do it. Once they're clear on what is expected of them, they can be counted on to do what they committed to do, and to accomplish it to the best of their ability. Awesome people don't "phone it in," meaning just show up to make the minimum possible effort. Self-disciplined people make decisions and stick to them. They don't start a diet on Monday and eat half a pie by Wednesday. They don't join a gym on January 2 and quit by January 16. Decide to build your self-discipline, and you'll be surprised how much more awesome you'll become!

**STEP
69**

Responsible people are on time or early.

They give themselves more than enough time to get where they're going so that if something unexpected happens, they will still be on time. Awesome people arrive early, get the best parking spots, have conversations with other early-arrivals, and sometimes discover opportunities that those who show up late aren't considered for and didn't even know were being made available. So do as the awesome responsible people do: set your alarm, build in plenty of margin just in case the unforeseeable happens, and improve your timeliness as you continue your journey toward awesome.

Awesome, responsible people have integrity.

This is a lot like honesty and reliability, but with a subtle difference. Maintaining one's integrity means *never* violating what you believe to be the line between right and wrong, good and evil, for any reason, regardless of how amazing the perceived prize may be. For example, if someone were to suggest that there was a way that you could cheat on your income taxes and save thousands of dollars, and were very unlikely to be caught, to cheat would be a violation of your integrity. For the person with integrity, being caught isn't the issue. Violating one's integrity is the point. No violation of integrity is acceptable for truly awesome people. Develop integrity by doing what you believe is right, no matter what.

Awesome people are good communicators

AWESOME PEOPLE CLEARLY express themselves so that others don't have to "de-code" what it is they're trying to say. They choose empathetic words when comforting someone who is down. They choose encouraging and inspiring words when motivating someone to action. They choose powerful words when they are rallying their team. When they have an idea to communicate, they are able to use their words, facial expressions, body language, tone of voice, and intonation to cast a vision that becomes a clear, actionable word picture in the minds and hearts of their colleagues.

Start encouraging everyone around you.

If someone is down, remind her that she has options she hasn't yet considered, that tomorrow is another opportunity to improve the situation. Sometimes all people really need is someone who will listen. Everyone can benefit from a word of encouragement. You can encourage anyone by pointing out something good about the person. You can say, "I really appreciate your cheerful attitude." Don't limit your encouragement only to those people with whom you are in a relationship. Giving a word of encouragement crosses all social and economic lines, from the chairperson of the board to the receptionist. Maya Angelou said, "People may not remember what you said, but they will remember the way you made them feel." Spreading encouragement is easy, free, and undeniably awesome!

Good communicators resist the temptation to get frustrated or angry with people around them who are frustrated or angry.

Responding to anger with more anger only makes the situation worse. Try not to dismiss or belittle the person either. When dealing with a person who is acting badly, step back and ask yourself what may be going on in that person's life. Think about the struggle or pain they may be secretly dealing with that leaves them without the capacity to handle much else. To avoid engaging in arguments, you can say things like, "You may be right," or, "You make a good point." With these positive statements, you're acknowledging and validating the person (without necessarily agreeing), which may just defuse their anger.

Awesome communicators know that accurately communicating a thought is <u>their</u> responsibility.

It is not the obligation of the listener to understand. They know that just because a person smiles and nods, doesn't mean they have really heard what was said or that they have a firm grasp of what is being communicated. When you need to explain something, do your best to put your thoughts in order first. Start at the beginning, make your points in a clear, concise, and logical order, and then ask questions of your listener to be sure that he or she has really heard and understood what you're trying to communicate. In cases where you're teaching or training people to do a specific task, you may even ask the person to repeat back to you what they've heard or what they'll need to do. Awesome people don't expect people to understand what they've said. They own responsibility for communicating their thoughts thoroughly.

Awesome communicators articulate clearly.

They don't mumble. They don't speak so softly that others have trouble hearing them. Good communicators use a confident tone and volume of voice, projecting loudly enough for the listeners to hear clearly every word that's spoken, but not sounding as though they're yelling. They make eye contact when speaking to others. Although they may look away to gather their thoughts, they focus on the people they're speaking to so as to minimize distraction by whatever may be happening in the area surrounding the conversation. They know that distractions cause people to lose their trains of thought, and to miss exchanges that can be important to the relationship or to the tasks at hand.

**STEP
75**

Awesome communicators think about what they want to say before they say it.

This minimizes the chances of an embarrassing moment of saying something inappropriate, something that could seriously damage the relationship (or get them fired), or something that could be considered a double entendre, or a slight or insult. If you're not sure yet what you want to say, remain quiet until the thought solidifies in your mind. Don't be just as surprised as everyone else about what pops out of your mouth. Awesome people are deliberate about their communication, and make the effort to build people up in every conversation, rather than pull them down.

Awesome communicators aren't afraid of having tough conversations.

They invest time before the conversation to carefully write out the points they want to make. This is not done with the intention of reading their notes to the other person, but to help them collect their thoughts ahead of time so they can say what they really intend and thereby avoid miscommunications that could worsen the situation or damage the relationship. They use these notes to help themselves stay on track when they have the conversation. Awesome communicators create and maintain good, healthy relationships because they care enough to invest the time in what can be difficult conversations. They share their thoughts and then listen carefully to the thoughts and feelings of others.

STEP
77

Awesome communicators are respectful, tactful, and diplomatic—especially when they have to bring correction or give advice.

Because they establish relationships before bringing correction, they are better able to do so without hurting the feelings of others. Consequently, others are more likely to receive correction from them. When they face a difficult conversation, they "sandwich" constructive criticisms in between honest compliments about things the person does well or positive character traits of the person so that they don't feel as though they've been beaten up. Awesome communicators never attack anyone personally. They use their healthy sense of humor to lighten conversations about difficult topics, letting the person know that the relationship is intact. Because awesome communicators put relationships first, others are more willing to learn from them.

STEP 78

Awesome communicators are excellent listeners!

Equally important in good communication is the skill of listening to others and really hearing what they have to say. Excellent listeners tend to be more receptive to new ideas because they listen, ask clarifying questions, and hear others out before offering opinions or suggestions. Consequently, other people are more willing to share their ideas with good listeners because they trust that they will be heard without ridicule or criticism. Awesome communicators understand that they can't know everything, so they're eager to listen to—and learn from—others. Because they listen as much as they talk, they often hear positions and opinions that they had not considered and ideas that they had not yet thought of. Awesome communicators tend to be more open-minded. They know that when people share ideas, collaborations can be born and positive results can be achieved. Awesome communicators tend to be the ones to whom opportunities for cooperative ventures and new collaborations present themselves.

**Awesome communicators
motivate others to action.**

They know that if they effectively communicate an idea along with how that idea can benefit the other person, it is more likely to be acted upon. This isn't manipulation; it's simply a matter of keeping the other person's needs and wants in mind. For example, rather than saying, "I want you to go with me," an awesome communicator might say, "I want you to go with me because I think you'll enjoy our time together." Notice that the awesome communicator has shifted the focus from what *he* wants to what he believes the other person will enjoy. When you want to motivate others to act, create a clear word-picture of what's in it for them.

**Awesome communicators
are responsive.**

When someone reaches out to them, they show that they
value the person and their relationship by responding as
quickly as possible. This doesn't mean that they accept
every invitation or do everything others want them to
do, but they respond and let people know one way or
another where they stand. By nurturing the relationship
in this way, they inspire others to come up higher in
these areas. They show others by their responsiveness
and listening skills what a good relationship looks like,
which can then be modeled by the other person and
shared again and again.

Awesome people are resourceful

WHEN PRESENTED WITH a challenge, resourceful people will figure out a way to get through it. Somehow, some way, they will see the situation resolved or get the job done. Resourceful people can be counted on to either figure things out or to find a "work-around" to get things done. These are the people who take charge in an emergency, who work extra hours when it's "crunch time," and who aren't able to truly rest until the work is done.

STEP 81

Resourceful people are hard workers.

They have good work ethic. They are either on time or early to work and to anywhere else they've committed to be. They don't get distracted by things that have nothing to do with the task at hand. They're often the last ones to leave, and they don't like to leave until the job is done. Because of their high level of work ethic, they are often offered promotions and opportunities that are not afforded to others. Awesome hard workers don't necessarily love their jobs or admire their bosses, but they do a good job because that's what they have been hired to do. This work ethic isn't limited to their work life, either; they apply this same effort in their personal lives.

STEP 82

Resourceful people are conscientious.

They want to do a good job at whatever they do. They love the sense of accomplishment that comes from taking on a challenge and resolving it. They even feel the same way about mundane tasks like cleaning and organizing. They take pride in their successes and completed tasks. They believe that if a job is worth doing, it's worth doing right. Resourceful people live by the old adage, "If you don't have time to do a job right the first time, how are you going to find time to fix it later?" Take pride in what you do. Every task you do has your fingerprints all over it, meaning that it is a representation of who you are as a person. Do as awesome people do: complete what you have to do in such a way that when people look at a job well done, they'll automatically think you did it.

Resourceful people are self-motivated.

They don't need to be reminded several times to get things done. Their motivation to do well comes from within. It's an internal drive that pushes them to get out of bed even when they would rather roll over and go back to sleep. Their self-motivation urges them to report for duty in life even when they don't feel up to it. It's that self-motivation which earns them the trust of family, friends, employers, and co-workers. Other people know that if they need something done, they can be assured it will be done if they give it to a resourceful, self-motivated person.

Resourceful people have scruples.

This means that they are very careful to avoid wrong-doing. Because they are conscientious, they care deeply about achieving good results and their scruples prevent them from taking shortcuts. For these people, a good result will never justify a wrong means of achieving it. It's not enough that they get a task done; they want to do it with excellence, the right way, and with transparency, so that if anyone looks behind the curtain of their achievement (or their life), they'll find nothing wrong, inappropriate, or untoward. Awesome scrupulous people are always trying to improve themselves and to do better in every area of their lives, and encourage others with their words and actions to do the same. On your journey toward awesome, become a person with morality and ethics that are above reproach—become known as a person with scruples!

Resourceful people are teachable.

They are eager to learn new ways of getting things done, new technology, and new ideas. Because awesome resourceful people are "get-it-done" people, they are always looking for new ways to be more efficient, more effective, and more productive. They read, take workshops, and listen to others, hoping to learn something from everyone they meet. Be like awesome, teachable people, and stay open to new ways of doing things.

Resourceful people are industrious.

When their work is done, rather than sit back and rest, they look around to see what else has to be done, and they ask others what they can do to help. They tend to be constantly busy working on something or searching for the next project. Resourceful, industrious people don't sit idle for long—if they sit at all. Be like awesome industrious people, and look around for ways that you can add value to the world.

Resourceful people are willing.

They're willing to try something they've never done before. They're willing to help others. They're willing to take on difficult tasks. They're willing to do the tough job no one else steps up to volunteer for. This willingness is an attitude. It is a stark contrast to those people who seem to be unwilling to do anything outside their comfort zone, routine, or job description. Many people are unwilling to try something they haven't done before out of fear of failure. They are unwilling to take on something that they perceive will involve a lot of effort. Awesome, resourceful people know that a willing friend, neighbor, co-worker, or employee is a treasure, so they strive to maintain an attitude of willingness.

Resourceful people are productive.

They don't just look for "busy work" to keep them occupied. They want to do things that produce good results. They like to work toward a finished product, whether it's making the bed, baking a cake, or building a successful business. They are driven by the satisfaction of standing back to see their efforts come to fruition. Resourceful people are motivated by the finished product. Their internal "scoreboard" of life keeps score of production, so anything that feels as though it will never be finished doesn't motivate and satisfy these awesome, productive people. When an awesome, productive person needs assistance, they seek out another awesome, productive person. Being awesome, resourceful and productive in your daily life could attract opportunities you could never have predicted.

Resourceful people are inventive.

They aren't limited to doing things the way they've always been done. They aren't afraid of trying new ways of approaching challenges and meeting needs. In so doing, they'll often come up with innovative ways to get things done. Awesome, resourceful people think outside the box. In fact, sometimes it can be a challenge to keep them *in* the box! They don't have to be told what to do and when to do it. They are willing to receive instructions, guidance, and advice so they can improve in all they do, but they don't have to be given step-by-step instructions and close supervision in order to get things done. To be awesome and inventive, challenge yourself to invent creative new solutions to the challenges you face.

**Resourceful people are adventurous
in the sense that they'll try different things
until they find what works for them.**

They know that there is usually more than one way to get something accomplished, so they aren't afraid to attempt and fail, step back and assess, and then try a different approach—sometimes over and over again until they get the results they are working toward. The essence of being resourceful is being willing to try, even if you fail. Be adventurous and unafraid to fail, and you will eventually succeed!

Awesome people are effective

AWESOME PEOPLE ARE effective. They get results. They can see the big picture, and are able to discern what needs to be done—as well as what shouldn't be done at all. They know that there is no bigger waste of time than to do something well that didn't need to be done at all. Awesome people are efficient, meaning they do what they do very well, they delegate what they don't do well, and they scratch things off the list that don't need to be done at all.

Effective people always have a plan.

These are the people who know what they want, and who invest time every day in going after it. They measure every opportunity against their goals and plans for their attainment. If something doesn't fit with their plan, they don't do it. If they do believe the opportunity will move them closer to their goals, they'll do it. This doesn't mean they are selfish or that they only care about their own plan. Rather, effective people know that there is a plan and purpose for everyone, and if they take an opportunity that doesn't move them closer to the plan for their life, they are not only derailing the train of their own life plan, but they could be "stealing" the opportunity from someone it was truly intended for. Be like the awesome, effective people who are deliberate about creating a plan, charting their course, and staying on track.

Effective people are observant, and are good at assessing clues.

They use their skills of observation to look for opportunities, for unmet needs, for the right people with whom to surround themselves, and for ways to enjoy life. They also use their skills of observation and assessment of clues to add value to their life and to the lives of others. For example, when someone in their life is grouchy, irritable, or reacts in a way that is out of proportion to the situation, rather than getting angry with that person, awesome people wonder what's wrong with him or her. They consider what they know as well as the clues that are available, and try to draw some kind of conclusion— not to be nosey or intrusive, but to determine if there is some way they can help that person. By honing your observation and clue assessment skills, you'll be honing your awesomeness.

STEP 93

Effective people think strategically.

They think carefully before making a serious decision. They think before entering a long-term relationship and before accepting a job offer. They think when planning a project, and they think before tackling a problem. Thinking situations through before acting may appear to be counter to efficiency and effectiveness. It may appear that a thinking person is wasting time in thought when they would be better served by launching into action. In truth, processing details beforehand helps effective people avoid pitfalls and minimizes the chances of error. Become an awesome strategic person and save yourself time, money, and heartache by thinking carefully and strategically before acting.

Effective people are organized.

They don't lose unrecoverable time every day searching for their keys. They don't waste time when trying to get ready or when beginning a project because their closets, garages, and workspaces are disorganized. They don't spend valuable time trying to remember forgotten passwords and online login information; instead, they store them neatly in a safe place or they memorize them. Organized people know that investing the time to clean out drawers, closets, workspaces, and storage areas is worthwhile because when they need something, they are be able to get to it without delay. Increase your awesomeness by improving the organization in every area of your life.

Effective people are prepared.

They prepare long before their preparations are needed rather than waiting until the last minute. They're never embarrassed by not being aware of something they should know. For example, an awesomely prepared person has recurring calendar reminders that list birthdays, anniversaries, and other important dates they'll want to remember year after year. This way, they never miss an opportunity to connect with and affirm the people they care about. An awesomely prepared worker invests the time to learn what they can about a potential employer or prospective client before the big meeting. Although it can be time consuming to prepare, in the long run the time spent preparing for what you know is ahead—and for the opportunities that may present themselves—is an investment in your future success. Awesome prepared people do all they can to never suffer the consequences of avoidable failure. Prepare for whatever it is you want, and you'll be far more likely to succeed in every endeavor, able to take advantage of opportunities that present themselves only to the well prepared.

Effective people are terrific time managers.

They treat each 24-hour period as though it were 24 pounds of gold that, once spent, can never be retrieved. They make certain that they are willing to exchange their precious time for whatever it is they'll be doing. When it comes to people, they invest the most time in those they care about most. They do not give their time and energy away to others, leaving little or none for those who are most valuable in their lives. They allot a certain amount of time to the tasks they have to do, and they stay on a task until it's completed. Effective time managers are skilled at building margins into their schedule so that they can quickly handle the inevitable interruptions of life, but then get back on task. Awesome time managers know that distractions that have nothing to do with their short-term and long-term goals are to be avoided at all costs. Keep track of your time and treat it like the precious asset it is, and you'll become an awesome, effective, time manager too!

**Effective people are
able to adapt to others.**

People who can adapt to those who are different than they are—such as people with different personalities, or with people of different cultures, skin color, religions, or economic status—are far more effective than those who don't easily adapt. Adaptable people don't waste time arguing with others or trying to persuade others to see things from their perspective or to do things their way. They are able to grasp the big picture and to assess differences from the standpoint of efficiency. As a result, they know when to adopt the ideas of others or to explain to others why they ought to do things differently in order to be more efficient and effective. They are willing to let others be who they are, without feeling the need to change them. Awesome adaptable people are willing to hear others out. Do that too, and you may learn something that makes you even more effective than you already are. And, in the process, you'll become even more adaptable.

Effective people are team players.

They don't feel the need to do everything themselves; in fact, they're usually good at recruiting others to help. They're typically good at training others on how to do things, overseeing them to make sure they really understand, and then keeping them focused on the task at hand. Awesome, effective team players know that their contribution to the family or the workplace is valuable, so they often don't seek acknowledgement, although they do appreciate it when it's given. They know that when the group succeeds, everyone involved benefits. Be like awesome team players, and believe that everyone's position in the family, workplace, neighborhood, and community is important. That way, you'll be helping to foster a greater sense of connection and cooperation among all.

Effective people never leave tasks half done or not done well.

They are thorough about everything they take on, whether it's baking cookies or negotiating a business deal. Effective people finish what they start, and they do their best to finish well. They consider everyone involved; they think about what people need and want, and about how their contribution fits into the big picture. They know that details can make the difference between success and failure in relationships, work, and every other aspect of life. Effective, thorough people can be counted on to make sure that their responsibilities are handled properly. Even if you're not detail oriented, work extra hard at being thorough at everything you take on and you will earn a reputation as an awesome, effective, and thorough person.

Effective people have a positive, willing, and cheerful, attitude.

They know that they can make up for whatever they may lack in other areas by having a good attitude. For example, the husband who forgets his wife's birthday has a much better chance of making things right with his wife if he has a positive, cheerful attitude. The employee with a willing attitude but who lacks formal education may still be chosen for a promotion over a highly educated person with a negative attitude. The great news about attitude is that *everyone* can choose to have a good attitude. It costs nothing, it requires no formal training, and a positive mental attitude can lead to total life transformation. Adopt a positive attitude by expecting good things to happen and by being willing to do your part to make them happen. Don't forget to tell your face to keep up with your choice to maintain a good attitude—a cheerful expression is the first thing other people see.

STEP
101

to Awesomeness

Awesome people are continuous learners. They are on a lifelong pursuit of never-ending self-actualization. It isn't about "fixing" themselves and it isn't about feeling compelled to "fix" others. They just know that as long as they're breathing, they're still in the game, and that there is still more value to mine from the experience train of their lives. They make it a point to learn something from everyone they meet—sometimes it's what *not* to do!

Awesome people know that new developments are always happening and technologies are always changing, so they never give up their desire to learn more, to teach others what they've learned, and to live an even more awesome life today than they did yesterday. For awesome people of all ages, awesome continuous learners like YOU, the future is exciting and bright!

CONCLUSION

NOW THAT YOU'VE learned about the key characteristics of awesome people and have gone through the 101 steps toward being the best you that you can be, it is your responsibility to open the door and step over into your new lifestyle by implementing these concepts.

You—and only you—can carry yourself with the confidence of knowing that you are awesome. You and only you can decide to live in awesomeness by taking on the 101 aspects of the characteristics that define your unique brand of awesomeness. You and only you can change your world by identifying, recognizing, and celebrating the awesomeness of the people within your influence.

When you help others see the awesomeness within themselves, you are literally changing the world. When you help other people live their best lives, they will naturally help others live their best lives, and so on and so on. Your awesomeness can start a ripple effect of awesomeness in your family, your neighborhood, your community, your workplace, and in your entire world.

This transformation is positive, meaningful, measurable, and sustainable…and it costs nothing! There is no negativity in awesomeness. Of course, that doesn't mean that bad things will never happen, but when they do, if you continue to live in your awesomeness, taking one step at a time through the challenges of life, the characteristics that make you awesome will see you through, sometimes to an even better outcome than you would have thought possible.

Everyone in your life may not be supportive of the transformation they see in you. Regardless, *do not stop.*

There are several reasons that someone would be less than supportive or downright critical of your determination to improve yourself and your life:

First, your positive transformation may reflect poorly on them. As you transform, becoming happier and living the life you were made for and deserve, others will be faced with a decision: to dare to believe that they too can be awesome, or to continue to live as they have. Sadly, many people aren't able to believe that there is awesomeness inside of them, or they're just not willing to make the changes necessary to embrace their awesomeness.

Second, your transformation to awesome may disrupt the dynamics of your relationship. For example, if two friends spend all of their time together gossiping about others or complaining about what's wrong in their lives, and one friend suddenly no longer wants to talk negatively about others, the other friend either has to shift the conversation to something else and find an activity that they can both enjoy, or they will drift apart. When you are living an awesome lifestyle, and have attracted friends who are living the same way, those who are negative and have only bad things to say will either adapt to the awesome new you, or they will move on to spend time with people who want to remain in go-nowhere negativity.

Third, if the other people in your life haven't yet identified and acknowledged those things that make them awesome, they may actually be envious of you. Hopefully their envy will spur them to action, but if they want the awesomeness that you have without being willing to do what you did to get it—taking the steps to fully actualize their awesomeness—they'll never quite get there.

Regardless of the reasons, the best you can do for the people who would rather pull you back into negativity or mediocrity is to give them a model of awesomeness to follow. Encourage them to develop their own awesomeness, and ultimately give them the grace to make their own choice without judgement. Refuse to give up your powerfully awesome future for the sake of.

If you find that you must move on, consider the fact that a person who truly loves and cares about you would want you to be your awesome self and live your best life—the same thing you want for them. A true friend will celebrate your awesomeness without a hint of jealousy because she'll know that she's awesome too, and that together you can complement each other's awesomeness to become exponentially more awesome together. When awesome people come together, exciting things can happen. The spark of two awesome people can light a powerful fire that influences others to embark on their own awesome journey.

You are awesome in your own unique way. I hope that you've seen your awesome self reflected in the pages of this book. There is not another YOU anywhere on planet Earth. There has never been anyone with your unique package of awesomeness. On your journey toward the destination of the fulfillment of your awesome life, continue to use these steps over and over again, and encourage others to use them. As you do, you will climb from one level to the next, toward the ultimate destination at the apex of AWESOME!

SHARE YOUR AWESOMENESS

WE WANT TO hear about your journey to awesomeness. What did you discover? What surprised you? Who joined you on your journey? What does your awesome lifestyle look like? What advice do you have for others? Let's continue the conversation at howtogettoawesome.com.

ABOUT THE AUTHOR

 Rhonda Sciortino went from foster care to millionaire by living out the 101 steps outlined in this book. Through her media appearances, speaking engagements, and mentoring, Rhonda helps others find and fulfill their awesome lives. Rhonda lives a truly great life complete with all five points of success which she defines as good relationships, good health, peace, joy, and financial provision. Additional information is available at www.rhonda.org.